JOSEPH and his of MANY COLOURS

illustrated by Leon Baxter

adapted by Philip Steele

Macdonald

Everybody in the land of Canaan had heard of Jacob. The old man had twelve strong sons, and more sheep than anyone could count. Jacob's sons were all fine boys, but there was one of them, Joseph, whom Jacob loved more than all the others.

One day Jacob decided to give Joseph a special present. He went to the best weaver in the land, and asked him to make a magnificent coat of soft wool. It was to be patterned in brilliant stripes: all the colours of the rainbow. Two weeks later, Jacob came to collect it.

'Your Joseph must be quite a lad,' said the weaver to Jacob.

'He is,' said Jacob proudly. 'One of the best. He's a bit of a dreamer, you know.'

'A dreamer?' The weaver grunted. 'I'd rather have a son who was a farmer or a good hunter. No good ever comes from dreamers.'

But Jacob shook his head. 'Well, maybe you are right – but it seems to me that dreams are sometimes sent to us by God. Be that as it may, I do know that if anyone deserves this present, it's my Joseph.'

So the coat was wrapped up, and Jacob took it home.

The next morning Jacob and his twelve sons were up early for breakfast. Joseph, as usual, was the last to arrive! Reuben and Simeon, the two eldest sons, were already mopping their dishes with a crust of bread. Benjamin, the youngest, sat to one side, fingering a wooden whistle he had carved himself. With a triumphant flourish, Jacob handed his gift to the latecomer.

'A coat! Oh, what a wonderful coat!' Joseph tried it on and tied the sash around his waist. The colours glowed in the morning sun.

'Look at him putting on airs,' whispered Levi.

'We have to make do with these old cloaks of goat skin,' moaned Judah enviously, 'and they're so itchy!' Joseph turned angrily on his brothers.

'Stop complaining, will you? I'll have you know that I had a dream last night. I dreamed that we were binding corn into sheaves. My sheaf stood up straight and tall, but your ones all bowed down to mine. What do you make of that, eh? One day you will all bow down to me, you mark my words!'

'Never!' chorused the brothers. 'You can keep your rotten dreams – and your fancy coat!'

Jacob was upset. He had only wanted to please God and make Joseph happy. Now the whole family seemed to be quarrelling. If only Joseph could keep his dreams to himself . . .

But that night Joseph had another dream. 'I was staring into the sky,' he explained to them all the next day, 'and I saw the sun and the moon and eleven stars all bowing down to me!'

Even Jacob was angry. 'You've gone too far this time, my boy! I suppose the sun and moon are meant to be me and your mother, and the eleven stars your brothers. Well, I'll have no high and mighty manners round here. Get to work, the lot of you!'

Simeon clenched his fists. 'Why should we work with your precious Joseph any more, father? He thinks he's too good for the likes of us.'

'Very well,' said Jacob wearily. 'You lads can go and see to my flocks at Shechem. Joseph, you stay here and help me mend that tent.'

The days passed, and Jacob had no word from his sons. Shechem was many miles away, and Jacob began to worry. He decided to send Joseph to see if they were all right.

Joseph took a donkey and rode for many hours. At last he found his brothers, in a lonely valley. They saw him coming – and decided to teach him a lesson.

'You lazy good-for-nothings!' Joseph greeted his brothers. 'Where have you –'

But before Joseph could utter one more word of complaint, Simeon knocked him over and pinned him to the ground.

'You're making my coat dirty!' squealed Joseph. 'Just you wait till father hears of this!'

'What shall we do to this teller of tales?' hissed Simeon. 'Shall we leave him behind in this pit? Or shall we get rid of him once and for all?' He held a hunting knife against his brother's throat.

'You mustn't kill your own brother,' said Reuben, 'or God will be angry with you. Leave Joseph in the pit without any water. That will teach him.' He rode off up the valley to search for some missing sheep – he could always set Joseph free when he returned, he decided.

While Reuben was away, the brothers tore Joseph's coat from his back. They tied his hands behind his back and threw him in the pit.

'Help! Help!' screamed Joseph. His brothers pretended not to hear him.

Just then some travelling merchants happened to pass by. They reined in their camels.

'And who is this noisy young man?' asked their leader, as he peered down into the pit.

'It's our brother, sir,' replied Simeon. 'A worthless young fool if ever there was one.'

'Well, he's worth something in the slave market in Egypt,' said the merchant. 'I'll buy him from you. Here, take twenty pieces of silver!' He threw a bag of coins to Simeon. Before the brothers realized what was happening, Joseph was bundled out of the pit and tied to a camel. Soon merchants, camels and Joseph had passed out of sight.

When Reuben returned he was frightened – and furious.

'You *sold* him?' he shouted. 'You sold your own brother? What shall we tell father?'

'Let's say Joseph was killed by a wild animal,' suggested Levi. 'We can dip his coat in goat's blood, so it looks as if he was attacked by a lion.'

When the brothers returned home with the blood-stained coat, Jacob was broken-hearted. His favourite son was dead – or so it seemed. The brothers felt guilty and miserable, and young Benjamin wept for days on end.

In the meantime, Joseph had arrived in Egypt. He was very unhappy. He missed his brothers, despite everything they had done to him. He prayed to God to look after him in this strange land.

The merchant sold Joseph to a man called Potiphar, who was captain of the guard. Potiphar was lazy, and only too pleased to let Joseph run his household for him. Everyone liked Joseph – and Joseph rather liked his new job. But Potiphar's wife thought Joseph was so handsome that she tried to make him fall in love with her. Joseph refused.

That made Potiphar's wife furious! How dare a slave turn her down? So she decided to get her own back, and worked out a plan. Then she stole Joseph's cloak, and ran with it to Potiphar.

'Joseph has attacked me!' she shouted. 'He grabbed hold of me, but I screamed and then he ran away. Look – he left his cloak in my hand. Have him thrown into jail!'

Potiphar was very upset. He liked Joseph – but he believed his wife. So Joseph, to his surprise, was taken to jail, and thrown into a cell.

Once again Joseph's luck seemed to have run out, but he knew God would look after him and he tried to stay cheerful. The governor of the jail took a liking to Joseph, and so did the other prisoners. When they were troubled by dreams, they would come to Joseph. He told them how the dreams were sent by God, and explained what they meant. He was always right.

Every night Joseph prayed that he would be set free. But for two whole years he stayed behind bars, staring out at the blue Egyptian sky.

One dark night, the Pharaoh of Egypt woke up with a start.

'Oh dear!' he gasped. 'I don't feel well!'

'There, there,' said his wife, 'it was probably something you ate.'

'No, I have been dreaming,' he groaned. 'I saw seven fat cows on the banks of the River Nile. Along came seven thin cows and gobbled them up. Then I saw seven fat ears of wheat eaten up by seven thin ones. What can this mean? Send for the priests and the wise men!'

The priests and the wise men were called, but nobody could explain the Pharaoh's dream. Then the royal butler spoke up.

'My lord,' he said, 'there is a slave in your jail who understands these things. When your Highness was er ... wise enough to put me in prison two years ago, this Joseph told me that I would be set free. And so I was!'

'Then bring the fellow to me!' wailed the Pharaoh.

18

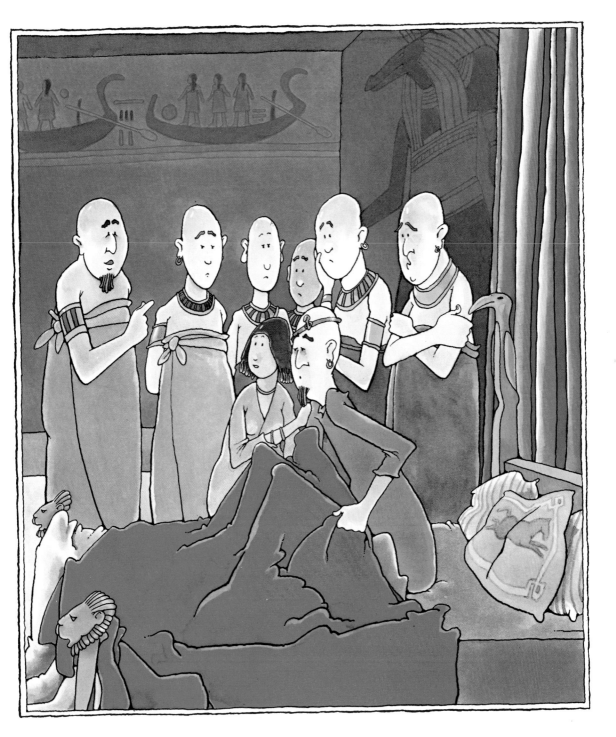

Joseph was dragged from his cell and brought before the Pharaoh. He bowed low as he was told of the terrible dreams. And then he spoke out loud and clear: 'The meaning is plain, my lord. God is telling you that Egypt will have seven years of good harvests, followed by seven years of famine and hardship. You should find a man to look after Egypt, who will store away some of the harvest in the good years, and so prepare for the bad years.'

The Pharaoh looked closely at Joseph.

'Young man,' he said, 'you are very wise for one so young. I shall make you Lord Governor, and *you* shall prepare us for the hard times ahead.'

And so Joseph became the most important man in Egypt. But whenever he heard the trumpets blowing in his honour, he remembered young Benjamin's wooden whistle. And whenever he put on his Governor's robes, he remembered his coat of many colours.

'Oh God,' he prayed, 'let me see my family again – I'm sorry I wasn't very nice to them. Send them to see me . . . soon . . .'

This story has been told in many different ways for more than three thousand years. It was first written down in a language called Hebrew. Since then it has been re-told in almost every language used in the world today.

You can find the story of Joseph in the Bible. This part of his life is in the Book of Genesis, Chapters 37, and 39 to 40.

There is a companion to this book, called 'Joseph and his Brothers'. It tells how Joseph came to meet up with his brothers once again.